"Many Christians want to read the Bible m[...] them are unsure of where to begin. Rach[...] the deep well of her own personal walk with Jesus, and she provides a realistic and helpful guide for any follower of Jesus to start a quiet time."

J.D. GREEAR, Lead Pastor, Summit Church, Raleigh-Durham, NC; Author, *Just Ask* and *Essential Christianity*

"I love this book because it does brilliantly two things that are rarely found together: it coaxes and coaches. First, it coaxes anyone who has never read the Bible for themselves, or anyone who has the lost the habit of doing so, to start. Its personal, engaging, realistic approach is motivating. Then it coaches you on doing that, starting small, getting bigger. It begins by demonstrating how to read God's word, but by the end you will be equipped to read for yourself. And along the way, you will have found how nourishing, life-giving and sustaining the Bible is. I strongly recommend this book!"

JAMES ROBSON, Principal, Oak Hill College, London

"Oftentimes, getting started is the hardest part of forming any new habit. And consistent Bible-reading is no exception. Rachel Jones has given us an excellent and accessible little book that delivers a big impact in our devotional lives. *The Quiet Time Kickstart* will help you build a rhythm and structure into your life that will energise (or re-energise!) the way you approach God's word, with biblically clear reflections and thoughtful questions. I highly recommend this book to anyone and everyone wanting to deepen their love for Scripture."

ADAM RAMSEY, Lead Pastor, Liberti Church, Australia; Director, Acts 29 Asia Pacific; Author, *Truth on Fire* and *Faithfully Present*

"We'd all love to be one of those model Christians who enjoy their hour-long daily workout of Bible study and prayer. But the reality is that many of us find it difficult to spend even a brief, unhurried time meditating on God's word and praying. And we can't go from spiritual couch potato to the Bible-reading equivalent of an Olympic weightlifter overnight. It takes time. Perhaps a personal trainer would help... Enter Rachel Jones. In her eminently sensible approach and with a quietly-optimistic-but-not-in-an-overpowering-way spirit, she guides us through a simple and do-able programme of Bible study and prayer. *The Quiet Time Kickstart* lasts only six weeks; the spiritual habits it helps us develop can last for a lifetime."

SINCLAIR B. FERGUSON, Professor of Systematic Theology, Reformed Theological Seminary; Author, *The Whole Christ*

"The living God has spoken to us in the Bible, and he continues to speak to us through the Bible. But starting to read the Bible can be a bit daunting. The good news is that *The Quiet Time Kickstart* walks you through the process, building up your confidence along the way. It does this not by talking about the Bible but by helping you to actually read the Bible for yourself. Rachel Jones doesn't assume that you know a lot of theology, but neither does she talk down to you. It's a great little guide to help you put in place some great lifelong habits."

TIM CHESTER, Crosslands Training; Author, *Enjoying Jesus*

The

Quiet Time

Kickstart

Six Weeks to a | **RACHEL**
Healthy Bible Habit | **JONES**

thegoodbook
COMPANY

The Quiet Time Kickstart
© The Good Book Company, 2025

Published by:
The Good Book Company

thegoodbook.com | thegoodbook.co.uk
thegoodbook.com.au | thegoodbook.co.nz | thegoodbook.co.in

Design by André Parker

ISBN: 9781802541366 | JOB-007873 | Printed in Turkey

Contents

A note from the author

Although all flaws in what follows remain my own, it seems only right to acknowledge that my thinking for this project has been most shaped by editing Gary Millar's little book *Read This First: A Simple Guide to Getting the Most from the Bible* (which would make a great follow-up if you're looking for more help with understanding Scripture) and by the excellent teaching of Tim Ward and others at Oak Hill College. This comes with gratitude to the whole Oak Hill community for helping me grow in my love for Jesus and my appreciation for his word over the last few years.

Welcome

For a long time, I wanted to be someone who runs. Over the years I'd watched several family members and friends lace up their running shoes, bound out of the house and down the road, and return sometime later looking sweaty but invigorated. *I'd like to be that person*, I thought. But I'd tried it once. Maybe twice. And running was not something I did.

A couple of summers ago, with a little more time on my hands, I decided to do the "couch to 5k" programme. It is what it sounds like—an app-based training programme that, over nine weeks, aims to get you from "couch potato" to someone who can comfortably run five kilometres. You start off running for 60 seconds and then walking for 90 seconds, on repeat. You have the voice of a friendly celebrity coming through your headphones, telling you when to run and when to walk and offering you generic but surprisingly effective encouragements. As the weeks progress, you gradually increase the amount of running and decrease the amount of walking, until you're jogging for 30 minutes solid.

And it... worked.

I found I enjoyed it. It was satisfying to make progress. It wasn't always easy—there were moments when my chest felt like it was bursting and my legs felt like dead weights. I had to fight the pre-run thought that I could just, well, not go running. But I liked how running made me feel after the fact: and sometimes even during the fact. I am now "a person who runs": someone who laces up their running shoes, bounds out of the house and down the road, and returns sometime later looking sweaty but invigorated.

Sorry if all that talk of running is immediately off-putting. My point is that I'm writing this guide for anyone who would like to be "a person who reads the Bible" (or "has a quiet time" or "does a daily devotional", or whatever else you'd like to call it). You know of friends or family members who make a hot drink and withdraw to a quiet room with their Bible in the morning, and emerge, sometime later, looking serene but invigorated. *I'd like to be that person*, you think. You've tried it once or twice or even a whole bunch of times over the years—or perhaps it was something you used to do regularly but now you're out of the habit. Reading the Bible is not something you do.

But it can be.

And that's where this little guide is designed to help. As with running, it's getting going with reading the Bible that's often the hard part; once you're in the habit, it will feel much more natural. And as with running, it can be helpful to start small and build up. We'll begin with just a couple of verses and a single thought—a three-minute devotional that anyone can make time and headspace for. Then we'll build up gradually to something a little closer to a "5k quiet time"—a comfortable level of Bible fitness that is going to nourish your spiritual health and wellbeing. Along the way you'll pick up some simple Bible-reading skills that will help you make sure you're listening carefully to what God has to say.

There's something important to say upfront, though: there isn't one standard "quiet time" that everyone needs to aim for. There's no single "right way" to read the Bible—and certainly no "ideal quiet time" length or style. In fact, the whole idea of doing a solo daily quiet time is a 100% non-compulsory part of the Christian life. It's a good idea—but nowhere does God command it of you. It's not about checking boxes or getting a streak.

This is a key difference between reading the Bible and running: reading the Bible isn't a "thing" you do; it's a conversation with the living God who loves you. The Creator God, who knit you together and saved you so you can live with him for ever, wants to speak to you—each and every day. Having a quiet time is about coming into his presence, basking in who he is, remembering how he feels about you, listening to what he has to say to you, and telling him what's on your mind.

That said, there will be days when you're feeling it and days when you're not. There'll be days when, spiritually speaking, your legs feel good and the sun shines and you smash your personal best—and days when you feel like you're plodding round the park in the rain. That's okay. The latter will feel less easy but will be no less good for you. You can trust that reading God's word and praying to him nourishes and sustains your soul, even if you don't get a "wow" feeling every day. And in God's kindness, there will be many days when he blows you away.

So lace up those shoes (or put on those slippers). Turn on the kettle. Open the Bible. And let's get started.

WEEK 1
Starting Small

Introduction

We start our Bible-reading journey in 1 Thessalonians. This is a letter written to the church in Thessalonica, and it's one of the earliest parts of the New Testament, written just 20 years or so after Jesus' death and resurrection.

Thessalonica was a city in a province of the Roman Empire called Macedonia (in what is Greece today). When the apostle Paul and his companions preached the gospel message there, lots of people (mostly non-Jews) responded by putting their faith in Jesus (Acts 17:1-10). But because of fierce opposition, Paul had to move on quickly, leaving behind a small church of brand new Christians.

When Paul writes this letter, his co-worker Timothy has recently been back to visit the Thessalonian church and has returned with good news (1 Thessalonians 3:6). So Paul is writing to tell them how happy he is to hear that they are going on well in their faith—and to encourage them to keep going.

Our reading plan this week starts small, with just a couple of verses to read each time. The aim is simply to open God's word every day and get something out of it—to end up smiling inside. But don't worry: the opening chapter of this letter is so enthusiastically upbeat that it won't be hard.

Day 1

Pray: *Ask God to speak to you today.*

The church receiving this letter is in the city of Thessalonica. But spiritually speaking, they are "in God the Father and the Lord Jesus Christ" (v 1).

As we read on, we'll see that these new Christians have had a rough start. But this truth is enough to hold them steady: they belong to "God the Father and the Lord Jesus Christ". The same is true of you and your church today.

Think about what kind of Father God is; and what kind of Lord Jesus is.

What words would you use to describe them?

That is who has got hold of you today!

How does that keep you steady?

Pray: *Tell God about any situations where you're feeling unsettled or shaken. Pray that knowing that you belong to him would make a difference to you.*

The first step is often the hardest... and you've done it. See you again tomorrow!

Day 2

Pray: *Ask God to fill your heart with faith, hope and love today.*

READ 1 THESSALONIANS 1:2-3

Paul is just so excited about these Thessalonian believers. When he remembers how the message of Jesus impacted their hearts, and how that played out in their lives, his joy and enthusiasm overflow!

Think of an example of how you've seen each of these things play out—either in your own life or in the lives of people in your church:

- Faith in Jesus --> working for the sake of others

- Love for Jesus --> labouring hard, even when it's tough

- Hope that Jesus will return --> endurance through difficult times

Pray: *Thank God for each of these examples, as Paul does in this passage.*

I so often jump straight into reading the Bible in my own strength. But we have no hope of truly understanding and being changed by God's word unless his Spirit helps us. That's why I've included these prompts to pray each day.

Day 3

Pray: *Thank God for how he's encouraged you through what you've read this week so far. Pray that he'd do that again today.*

Paul is continuing to tell the Thessalonian Christians why he hasn't stopped thanking God for them.

READ 1 THESSALONIANS 1:4-5a

(to the end of the first sentence)

The Christians in Thessalonica have been chosen by God to be his people. The reason Paul knows that is because, when he preached the message of Jesus to them, the words didn't just pass them by. They had a powerful effect, as the Holy Spirit convinced the Thessalonians that Paul's message was true.

The "message of Jesus" is what we usually call the "gospel": the good news that Jesus died and rose again, so that we can have our sins forgiven and our relationship with God restored.

Think back to a time when the gospel hit you powerfully and changed your heart in some way. That right there is evidence that you are "loved by God" and "that he has chosen you"! *How does that change your perspective on what lies ahead of you today?*

Pray: *Thank God that he loves you and has chosen you, and ask him to keep working in you by his powerful Spirit, so that you continue to change.*

Day 4

Pray: *Ask God to reveal what he has for you in his word.*

READ 1 THESSALONIANS 1:5b-7

Becoming a Christian hadn't made life easier for these believers; in fact, it had made life harder. We discover in chapter 2 that the "severe suffering" they endured was at the hands of friends and neighbours who were against Jesus (2:14-15).

Yet all that didn't stop the Thessalonians from *welcoming* the message, and it certainly couldn't stop the Holy Spirit from filling them with joy.

By suffering in this way, the Thessalonians weren't just being like Paul; they were being like Jesus himself.

How have you known joy in the midst of suffering?

Be encouraged: this too is a sign that you are loved and chosen by God (1:4).

Pray: *Pray for Christians you know (or know of around the world) who are suffering. Ask God to fill them with joy as they remember that they are walking in Jesus' footsteps.*

These verses remind me of this description of Jesus' joyful perseverance through suffering: "For the joy that was set before him he endured the cross, scorning its shame, and sat down at the right hand of the throne of God" (Hebrews 12:2). I've always loved that picture of his resolve on our behalf.

Day 5

Pray: *God is with you and is ready to speak. Ask him to help you hear.*

Big news travels fast. Have you ever been about to tell someone your exciting announcement, only for them to jump in first: "Hey, I heard that you..."? Paul can relate to that.

READ 1 THESSALONIANS 1:8-10

As Paul travels around preaching the gospel, news of the Thessalonians' conversion has got there before him. Everyone's talking about it. And with good reason: the Thessalonians had done a dramatic 180-turn: from worshipping empty idols to serving the true and living God. They'd put their hope in Jesus, the Son of God who can rescue us from God's wrath—his judgment of sin that sinners deserve.

Turning from idols; serving the true God; waiting for Jesus.

How has God enabled you to do each of those things? In what ways do you still want to grow in them?

Pray: *Thank Jesus that he rescues us. Pray that your turning, serving and waiting would have an impact on non-Christians you know, just as they did for the Thessalonians.*

One week and one chapter down! Keep at it.

What about the Weekend?

This plan has five readings a week in case you need a day or two to catch up (because, well, life happens). But if you've managed a clean sweep so far and are hungry for more before Monday, why not...

- read 1 Thessalonians 1 all the way through. What strikes you? You could try journalling your thoughts, or writing out a prayer in response, or memorising one particular verse that you'd like your heart to remember.

- read the passage that's going to be preached in your church this Sunday. What did you find interesting? Exciting? Surprising? Confusing? Ask God to speak to you and your church family as you meet together.

Thoughts, questions and ideas:

WEEK 2

A Steady Pace

Introduction

This week, we're continuing into chapter 2 of 1 Thessalonians. It's almost like one big "I love you" from Paul to the Thessalonian Christians. He'd had to leave them in a hurry because of intense opposition. (You can read about it in Acts 17:5-10.) So now he assures them that his absence is not because he doesn't care. He reminds them of how he acted when he was with them. He's desperate for them to keep trusting the message he brought to them, even though things are tough and their faith is still very new.

Now that we're getting into a rhythm, we'll move to reading a handful of verses each time. And we'll begin to focus a little more on how to understand the passage itself.

The first question to ask ourselves when we read the Bible is, "What does it say?" It sounds obvious, but it's so easily overlooked! We need to look carefully at the words in front of us, to make sure we're not assuming we know what it says already or jumping to conclusions. And it's helpful to notice how it says what it says. So each day, you'll see that I've written a question or two that get your eyes looking at the passage and noticing what's there.

But be reassured: God wants to make himself obvious—he wants to speak to you! So let's tune in and listen...

Day 1

Pray: *It's a new week, with countless new mercies from God in store. Ask him to shower them on you as you read today.*

When Paul and Silas preached the gospel in Philippi, they were beaten up and imprisoned (v 2; Acts 16:19-24). Yet once they'd got out, they went to Thessalonica and did the exact same thing: preached the gospel.

What was motivating Paul to share the gospel in Thessalonica, despite the danger (1 Thessalonians 2:2-4)?

Life has got harder for the Thessalonians since they became Christians; but Paul is not a religious conman who tricks gullible people into joining his cult. He's God's approved messenger. So the Thessalonians can have confidence in what he says—and so can we.

When do you find it hard to trust what God says (either because of your circumstances or the content of the message)? Whose example encourages you?

Think about situations where you have the opportunity to speak for Jesus. *Could you say the same thing about your motives as Paul says about his?*

Pray: *Talk to God about the corners of your heart where you doubt God's word or your motives aren't right. Ask for God's help, forgiveness and courage.*

It's often helpful to read the passage twice, if you can. I usually pick up on way more things as I read a second time!

Day 2

Pray: *Lord, show me more of who you are. Amen.*

Paul is still reassuring these Thessalonians that he cares about them, by reminding them of his visit. It's possible he's doing this because some people in Thessalonica have been throwing unfair accusations at Paul in his absence.

READ 1 THESSALONIANS 2:5-7a

List all the things that Paul and his co-workers did not do when they were in Thessalonica.

Instead, they were "like young children" (v 7). *In what ways is being "like young children" the opposite of the things you listed?*

Paul is an apostle: someone "approved by God to be entrusted with the gospel" (v 4). That gave him a level of authority and importance. But Paul wasn't throwing his weight around. Instead, he was like a young child: no faking or flattery, just genuine humility and honesty.

That is the kind of servants of whom God approves. In fact, that is the kind of servant whom God became: "The Son of Man came not to be served, but to serve, and to give his life as a ransom for many" (Matthew 20:28).

Pray: *Who do you know who serves Christ with a similar attitude to Paul's? They are the real deal! Thank God for them now.*

Day 3

Pray: *Lord, thank you that you are my Father in heaven, ready to speak and ready to listen to me. Please do that now. Amen.*

READ 1 THESSALONIANS 2:7b-12

In what ways did Paul act like a parent to the Thessalonian Christians? What was motivating him?

Several of my friends have become parents over the last few years. Each new baby reminds me of this: parenting is really hard work. And yet it's never grudgingly done (most of the time!); it comes from a place of deep love.

So too with Paul. He loved the Thessalonians and did everything he possibly could to enable them to understand and live out the gospel—starting with leading by example.

Paul is reminding these believers of how he did all the things he's about to tell them to do in this letter. He's a gospel minister worth listening to, and worth imitating.

God has called you into his kingdom and glory (v 12)! What an incredible privilege. *What would it look like to live today in a way that is worthy of that? Which element of Paul's example do you most want to copy?*

Pray: *Ask for God's help.*

Day 4

Pray: *Father, thank you that you've called me into your kingdom! Show me more of what it means to live with you as my King. Amen.*

READ 1 THESSALONIANS 2:13-16 ←

What was the proof that the word of God was at work in the Thessalonian believers (v 14)?

One thing to look out for in letters are the linking words: like "for", "because", "so", "therefore" or "but". They show us the flow of the argument.

Paul's courageous words and loving deeds bore fruit: the Thessalonians embraced his message as being from God. But the word of God was doing something in them too. That's why, like the people who became Christians before them in Judea, they were willing to follow Jesus even though it meant suffering at the hands of their neighbours and friends.

It's tempting to think that our culture is becoming increasingly hostile to Christianity; and maybe it is. But accepting the gospel has always involved a cost—just as it cost Jesus his life in the first place. The comfort for the Thessalonians, and for us, is that those who sneer at Jesus and his people will not have the last laugh.

When have you felt the cost of following Jesus? Thank God that your perseverance shows that his word is at work in you.

Pray: *Pray for Christians you know who face difficult situations because of their faith.*

Day 5

Pray: *God's word is at work in those who believe (v 13). Pray that it would be at work in you today.*

READ 1 THESSALONIANS 2:17-20

Why is Paul so desperate to visit the Thessalonians again (v 17, 19)?

Paul had to make a hurried exit from Thessalonica, and he hasn't been back. But he wants the Thessalonians to know that he loves them deeply. Indeed, they are his pride and joy.

All of us take pride and joy in something—and perhaps feel a bit guilty about it. But by investing in these new Christians, Paul is setting his hopes on something that will outlast this age: the Thessalonians and their new-found faith are "the crown in which we will glory in the presence of our Lord Jesus Christ when he comes". When we labour hard in Jesus' service, we can know that one day it will prove to have been worthwhile.

Too often for me it's "out of sight, out of mind". I'm so challenged by Paul's emotional investment in these Christians.

What kind of things are your pride and joy? Are they things that you will be glorying in on the day that Jesus comes again or will they have faded into insignificance?

Pray: *Thank God for the believers who are your glory and joy. Ask God to realign your priorities to the things that matter most.*

Another week, and another chapter. Be encouraged: you're making great progress!

The Weekend Page

Take the weekend to catch up or to...

- read 1 Thessalonians 2 all the way through. What strikes you?
  You could try journalling your thoughts, or writing out a prayer in
  response, or memorising one particular verse that you'd like your heart
  to keep remembering.

- read the passage that's going to be preached in your church this
  Sunday. What did you find interesting? Exciting? Surprising?
  Confusing? Ask God to speak to you and your church family as you
  meet together.

WEEK 3

Lengthening
Our Stride

Introduction

You're three weeks into our reading plan and still going strong. Well done!

This week we'll focus on lengthening our stride, by taking in a little bit more of the Bible each day. We're also going to work harder at taking truths from the passage and applying them to ourselves. Key to that is the question "Why?"

Last week we were focusing on "What does it say?" This week it's "*Why* does it say that?" Every word in the Bible has been carefully chosen by its human author—and inspired by its divine author, God—for a particular purpose. Each time we read part of the Bible, we can be confident that God has put these words in the Bible in order to *do something* for the people reading—both the first readers back then, and us today.

So, once we've figured out what a passage is saying on a basic level, we can consider why it's saying it. In other words, what did Paul want the Thessalonians to do, or think, or feel, as result of reading these verses? And, connected to that, what does God want us to do, or think, or feel, as a result of these words?

Why does God want me to hear this? It's as we consider this question that God's word powerfully changes the realities of our lives.

This week we reach the halfway mark of 1 Thessalonians, which is also a turning point in the letter. In the first half (1:1 – 3:10), Paul has been telling the Thessalonians why he's giving thanks for them. In the second half, from chapter 4 onwards, Paul is going to give the Thessalonians instructions on "how to live in order to please God" (4:1). Between these two sections, as a kind of bridge, we listen in on Paul's prayer (3:11-13). It draws together lots of the themes from both halves: love, holiness and perseverance, all with eyes fixed on Jesus' second coming. Let's get going.

But be reassured: God wants to make himself obvious—he wants to speak to you! So let's turn the page, tune in, and listen...

Day 1

Pray: *Talk to God about how you're feeling and invite him to speak into those emotions now.*

Let's recap: Paul had preached the gospel in Thessalonica. Some people had believed, but they immediately came under fire for their new faith. Paul was chased out of town and wasn't able to go back. Understandably, he was worried...

READ 1 THESSALONIANS 3:1-5

What did Paul decide to do (v 2, 5)? Why did he do that (v 3)?

Why is he telling the Thessalonians about it now, do you think?

Following Jesus has made life harder for the Thessalonians. Paul doesn't want them to give up (v 3). He knows that Satan—"the tempter"—would love nothing more than for them to quit and is using opposition to try and tempt them away from the faith (v 5).

But Paul also knows this: both he and the Christians in Thessalonica—and indeed all God's faithful people— are "destined" for trials (v 3). None of this is a surprise.

If I'm struggling to focus or to get into a passage I sometimes read it aloud. It helps me think about the emotions behind the words as I try to express them.

It's all part of God's plan. Life is hard now, but when we endure in faith, we're destined for glory. That's the way life looks for a follower of Jesus on this side of his return.

Paul had told the Thessalonian Christians about that when he was with them. Now he's telling them again for the same reason: so they'll keep following Jesus and not give up.

When are you tempted to give up following Jesus? How does being aware of Satan's involvement, and God's masterplan, help you to keep going?

Pray: *Speak to your Father about your answers.*

We're not left to endure alone though. We're following in the footsteps of Jesus, and he's with us by his Spirit! Romans 8:18-30 has long been precious to me.

Day 2

Pray: *"Speak, LORD, for your servant is listening."*
(1 Samuel 3:9)

Paul has sent Timothy to check in on the Thessalonians. Timothy has just got back to Paul with news...

READ 1 THESSALONIANS 3:6-13

What is Paul giving thanks for (v 6-9)? On a scale from 1-10, how would you rank his enthusiasm?

What is Paul praying for (v 10-13)?

The Thessalonians are doing well, and that's a cause for celebration. But following Jesus is more of a marathon than a sprint—and the most important thing isn't how well you start; it's whether you make it to the finish (v 13).

So Paul is praying that he'll be able to return to the Thessalonians so that he can teach them the things that he didn't have time to cover on his first visit (v 10). These are the things he prays for in verses 11-13, and that he's going to explain in chapters 4 – 5. Since he can't be with them in person, he'll remind them of the headlines via this letter.

Why does Paul tell the Thessalonians that he is praying these things for them, do you think?

How does it make you feel to know that God is at work doing these things in your life too?

Pray: *Use 3:12-13 to pray for yourself and for Christians you know.*

Why not take a leaf out of Paul's book, and tell someone what you've been praying for them? (I'll admit, I often feel awkward saying that kind of thing—but what I try to remember is how much I always love hearing it!)

Day 3

Pray: *Tell God three things you're grateful for right now; then ask him to meet with you as you read.*

What is the goal of a Christian, day by day (v 1)?

In the verses that follow, Paul tells the Thessalonians how to do that in one specific area.

What is Paul's message? Why does he want them to hear that?

Sexual immorality—that is, any sexual activity outside of the context of marriage—is not fitting for those who know God. God hates it, and it harms other people too (v 6).

This is hard for us to hear in the 21st century. But it was hard back then too. The culture in Thessalonica was as sex-saturated as our own; worship in pagan temples often involved sexual activity. We can assume that Paul was only writing this because there were believers in this church who were not avoiding sexual immorality. Maybe that's you, too.

But that's not who we are anymore: we have been called, personally, by a holy God, who now lives in us by his Holy Spirit (v 8). He will answer our prayers and strengthen our hearts in the face of temptation (3:13).

Which of the truths in this passage do you find most helpful in the fight against sexual sin?

Pray: *Confess your failures; enjoy God's full and free forgiveness; ask for his help.*

Day 4

Pray: *Your heavenly Father is listening. What do you want to say?*

READ 1 THESSALONIANS 4:9-12

What encouragement does Paul have for the Thessalonians in verses 9-10?

Notice how he tells them to "mind their own business and work" right after he's told them to love one another "more and more" (v 11-12).

Why does he do that, do you think? What's the link?

Love for God's people is an essential of the Christian life (remember 3:12!). It's something that God himself teaches us to do—in his word and by his Spirit in our hearts. God saved your brother or sister because he loved them, so it pleases him when you love them too— and there's always room for more love (4:10)!

For the Thessalonians, there was a specific way that love needed to be shown. It seems some of them were so excited that Jesus was going to come back immediately that they'd given up work, and were either sponging off others or just generally making a nuisance of themselves (see 2 Thessalonians 3:6-13). And that's not loving, nor is it a good look to those outside the church (1 Thessalonians 4:12).

How have you seen God helping you to love your church family? In what specific ways do you want to grow in this?

Pray: *Talk to God! You could...*

- *thank God for brothers and sister you love.*

- *ask for his help to love people you find it hard to love.*

- *pray that non-Christian friends, colleagues and neighbours would be impacted by "your daily life" today.*

I find it so helpful to shape my prayers around what I've just read. It's often as I'm praying that the Spirit works the truths into my heart.

Day 5

Pray: *How's your heart? Slow and sluggish, light and free, or somewhere in between? Tell the Lord and ask him to fill you with hope that's overflowing.*

Now Paul changes topic. It seems likely that he's responding to a concern raised in Timothy's recent update...

READ 1 THESSALONIANS 4:13-18

The Christians knew that Jesus was going to return to establish his rule on earth—an event they were eagerly awaiting. But some believers had died in the meantime—and, according to their old pagan way of thinking, that was that. They were gone. Dead and buried. No hope. Never to see Jesus' kingdom.

How does Paul answer that worry? Read verses 14-17 again, trying to imagine every detail.

I find it kind of hard to imagine, if I'm honest. But we can be confident that this really will happen in the future because Jesus died and rose in history (v 14). If God could raise him, he can raise us. And then at last we'll be with Jesus, our Saviour—the one who we've been following all this time.

Why does Paul want the Thessalonian Christians to hear this? What does he want them (and us) to do as a result (v 13, 18)?

Who could you encourage with these words today? Could you pray for a Christian who might be in particular need of this encouragement, and then send them a message?

Pray: *Thank Jesus for this glimpse of your future. Try to use each detail of verses 14-17 to help yourself to praise him.*

Our passages will be a little longer next week. If you're doing your quiet times first thing, could you set your alarm 5 minutes earlier? You'll barely notice (probably...).

The Weekend Page

Again, either take the weekend to catch up or...

- read 1 Thessalonians 3 – 4 all the way through. What strikes you? You could try journalling your thoughts, or writing out a prayer in response, or memorising one particular verse that you'd like your heart to keep remembering.

- read the passage that's going to be preached in your church this Sunday. What did you find interesting? Exciting? Surprising? Confusing? Ask God to speak to you and your church family as you meet together.

WEEK 4

Overcoming Hurdles

Introduction

We're four weeks in, and ready for a challenge. This week we'll be finishing up 1 Thessalonians before flying through its sequel, 2 Thessalonians. Much of what we read will concern Jesus' second coming: "the day of the Lord".

And due warning: some of the passages of this week are hard. I mean that in two senses.

First, some of it is hard to understand. 2 Thessalonians contains what is possibly the most baffling chapter in the whole New Testament. There will be points where we're left wondering, "What on earth is Paul talking about?" And the answer is "Nobody's really sure".

When we come across passages like that in the Bible, a good question to ask is "What's the big picture?" We don't need to nail down every detail first time through. Instead, aim to get the gist of what's going on and concentrate on what you do understand. In any passage, we're sure to find nuggets of gold that move us to worship.

And take heart: once we've got to the end of this week, you'll know that you can tackle even the Bible's weirdest and wildest sections!

There's another way in which this week might be hard, though: some of it is hard to hear. We'll be confronted with difficult truths about God's judgment and what that means for people we know and love. When we come across passages like that, we'll aim to be honest and humble, bringing our questions to God and genuinely seeking to hear his response.

Here's the principle to take away though: yes, some days we'll close our Bibles feeling more confused than when we started—and that's okay. There's always tomorrow. So don't let one day's confusion stop you from opening your Bible the next day. We can be confident that as we keep coming back to God's word, day after day, little by little, he will continue to do his work in us.

Day 1

Pray: *It's a fresh week! In what ways do you feel that you need a fresh start with the Lord? Speak to him about them.*

At the end of chapter 4, Paul was comforting the Thessalonians by explaining that death is not the end: one day Jesus will come back. In the meantime, we need to live as if we're expecting it.

READ 1 THESSALONIANS 5:1-11

Paul is comparing non-Christians (who belong to the night/darkness) and Christians (who are children of the light/day).

What are some of the differences between them?

Why is Paul making this contrast—what does he want the Thessalonians to do as a result (v 6-8, 11)?

Paul is using lots of overlapping images here. The big message is that the day of the Lord is coming—and in fact, Christians already "belong" to it (v 8). We're already in the light. We're no longer ignorant of God, groping around in the darkness of sin. He's chosen us for salvation (v 9). *So,* says Paul, *don't live as if you belong to the night. Be ready for the day.* Don't be distracted by the things of this world, intoxicated by all that they seem to offer. Instead, be "awake and sober", or self-controlled (v 6).

What worldly things do you sometimes look to for a sense of "peace and safety" (v 3)?

What would it look like to regard those things with sober eyes?

We will know peace and safety on the day of God's judgment because our Lord Jesus Christ "died for us so that ... we may live together with him", today and for ever (v 10). Thank you, Jesus!

Pray: *Stand up. Imagine yourself putting on faith and love as a breastplate and the hope of salvation as a helmet. Ask God to make you alert to opportunities to exercise faith, love and hope today.*

I find it so easy to get sucked into earning, saving and spending, as though my peace, safety and joy depend on it. This passage is such a helpful wake-up call!

Day 2

Pray: *Thank God for all that you've heard him say to you through 1 Thessalonians. Ask him to speak to you again today.*

We've reached the last stretch of this letter. Brace yourself for some quick-fire final instructions!

READ 1 THESSALONIANS 5:12-28

Paul has lots to say about how we relate to our church leaders (v 12-13), other Christians (v 14-15), the Lord himself (v 16-28), and the Spirit as he addresses us in our church gatherings (v 19-22).

There are at least 17 things we're told to do (or not do) here. The commands come so thick and fast that it's almost impossible to take them in all at once. So, let's try meditating on just one.

Read verses 12-22 again, asking the Spirit to highlight one particular command that he wants to impress upon your heart today.

Reread that sentence or phrase over and over, emphasising a different word each time.

Close your eyes and keep running it through your mind.

Let that turn into prayer: thanking God for how he's helped you obey, repenting of the ways you've failed, receiving God's forgiveness and asking for his help to live this out today.

Reread verses 23-24 and turn that passage into prayer too.

And be encouraged: God himself is working to sanctify you, through and through. He desires to keep you trusting Jesus, so that when he returns you will stand before him, completely and utterly free from blame. And God is faithful; he will do it!

You've finished 1 Thessalonians! As a friend of mine likes to say when we do things well, "Praise God and pat the donkey". (You being the donkey...)

Day 3

Pray: *Thank God that he has lots in store to say to you as you start this new book. Ask him to speak!*

The organisation Open Doors estimates that around the world, one in seven Christians are persecuted for their faith. It was to believers facing these kinds of challenges that Paul wrote 2 Thessalonians.

READ 2 THESSALONIANS 1:1-12

What does Paul say it is right for him to do, and why (v 3-4)?

These new Christians are persevering in their faith, despite intense pressure—it sounds crazy, humanly speaking. But we're not speaking humanly. Their faith is evidence that God is at work in them: through Christ, he has declared them "not guilty" and will one day bring them fully into his kingdom (v 5).

What else does Paul reassure the Thessalonians will happen in the future (v 6-10)?

How do you think they'd have felt hearing this? How do you feel?

These are frightening verses for those of us who know non-Christians whom we love. But they're written to encourage oppressed believers that God has not

If reading bigger chunks of text is a challenge, you could try listening to an audio Bible and following along. You can listen for free via the YouVersion Bible App.

abandoned them. Right now, in the world's eyes, they look weak and downtrodden. But one day, Jesus will be revealed. Those who shunned him will themselves be shunned. Jesus will be glorified. And we will stand and marvel. That is the endpoint your life is heading to.

With all that in mind, what does Paul ask God to do for the believers in the present (v 11-12)?

What goodness do you desire, or what deed is the Lord prompting you to do?

He wants to bring it to fruition!

Pray: *Thank God for the faith, love and perseverance that he is working in your life, and the lives of Christians you know. Pray that by his power he will help you to persevere in trusting him and loving others—and that all of it would bring glory to Jesus.*

Day 4

Pray: *Father, open my eyes that I may see wonderful things in your word. (Psalm 119:18)*

READ 2 THESSALONIANS 2:1-17

There's a lot going on here! Let's step back and consider the bigger picture.

Why is Paul writing this—what problem is he addressing (v 1-2)?

It might seem an odd concern to us. But the Thessalonians were new Christians living in wild and uncertain times. *Maybe the wars, famines and plagues around us are signs that God's judgment is already here,* they seem to have wondered. And if so, why hadn't Jesus shown up? Was he not going to save them after all?

Why does Paul say that it's not possible for the day of the Lord to have already come (v 3)?

Verses 5-12 give more detail about this "man of lawlessness", the rebellion he'll lead, and how he'll ultimately be overthrown by the Lord Jesus (all of which Paul had apparently already told the Thessalonians about in person, v 5!).

But we're still left with some obvious questions: Who exactly is the man of lawlessness? Who or what is holding him back? What exactly will his "rebellion" involve? (And since when did God start deluding people?!)

The short answer is that we're not really sure. Paul could be talking about: a historical figure who defiled the temple in Jerusalem later in the 1st century; or a repeated pattern throughout history of those who work against the gospel; or false teachers who lead Christians astray; or an "Antichrist" who is yet to appear.

Thankfully, the main take-home of this chapter is still clear...

What is the good news for the believers reading this (v 13-14)?

Don't miss how incredible this is!

What is Paul's big action point for them (v 15)?

What parts of the Bible's teaching might you be at risk of losing grip on or being unsettled by? How can you make sure that you "stand firm and hold fast"?

Pray: *Use verses 13-17 to thank God and ask for his help.*

Day 5

Pray: *The Lord is with you. Ask for his help to hear and understand.*

Paul wraps up his letter by addressing a few "other matters".

READ 2 THESSALONIANS 3:1-5

The big message of chapter 2 was to hold on to God's truth, as given to us by Paul (and the other Bible writers). But it's not simply about believing the Bible's claims—it's about doing what it commands (v 4). So next, Paul zeros in on one particular command that seems to have been an issue for the Thessalonians.

READ 2 THESSALONIANS 3:6-18

What seems to have been the problem?

Why is it important for believers who are able to work to do so, do you think?

It's not that these people want to work and aren't able to. (Elsewhere Paul tells us to look after those who cannot support themselves—see 1 Timothy 5:3, 16.) Nor are they just lazy; they are actively disruptive! Maybe they are so convinced that the day of the Lord has come that they think that work is not worth the effort (2 Thessalonians 2:2). And by spouting these ideas, they are contributing to the misunderstanding that is unsettling the rest of the church.

What does Paul command such Christians to do (3:12)?

What does Paul command the rest of the church to do (v 6, 13, 14-15)? What's your instinctive response to that command?

It sounds harsh, but a Christian who wilfully ignores what God clearly commands puts both themselves and others in danger. So it is loving to warn them, so that their shame might lead to repentance (v 14-15).

Pause to consider: are there ways in which you need to take action to obey one or other of these commands?

Pray: *Ask for God's help to "continue to do the things" he commands (v 4) and ask for his peace (v 16).*

You've read another book. Take a moment to appreciate how far we've come!

WEEK 4

The Weekend Page

Once more, either take the weekend to catch up or...

- read 1 Thessalonians 5 and 2 Thessalonians all the way through. What strikes you? Journal your thoughts, write out a prayer in response, or memorise one particular verse.

- read the passage that's going to be preached in your church this Sunday. What did you find interesting? Exciting? Surprising? Confusing?

WEEK 5

Switching
the Terrain

Introduction

So far, we've been reading New Testament letters. This week, we're mixing things up with some Old Testament narrative. Think of it like switching from running on an athletics track to a woodland trail. Our legs will do the same basic movement, but things will look and feel a little different.

This brings us to a third question that will help you hear what God is saying to you in any particular passage. Along with the what and the why, it's also helpful to ask, "Where are we?" Or "Where does this fit?" The word often used for this is "context".

If someone asks, "Where are you?" you could answer on a number of levels. You might say "In the living room" or "At home" or "On Planet Earth," or something in between, depending on who is asking (and how helpful you are trying to be).

The same is true when we're thinking about the "where" of a Bible passage.

We can think about where the passage fits in with the overall story or message of the book it's in—how it connects with what's come before and what's coming next.

We can also think about where the passage fits in the big story of the Bible as a whole—how it connects with what's come before and what's coming next.

In particular, Jesus said that the whole Bible is about him (Luke 24:27; John 5:39-40). So it's always worth asking, "Where's the route to Jesus?" Old Testament passages will constantly be "pointing forward", giving us glimpses and shadows of who he is and how he came to save us.

We'll be putting all that into practice in the book of Ruth. It's a beautiful story of love and loyalty—not just between its human characters but also between God and his people. And that makes it a heart-warming read for followers of Jesus today.

Day 1

Pray: *Talk to God about how you're feeling today and ask him to speak into that through his word.*

READ RUTH 1:1-5

What choices do Elimelek and his family make—and how do things turn out for them?

Where are we in Bible history (v 1)?

"The days when the judges ruled" are described in the previous book, Judges (read Judges 21:25 for a one-verse summary). Basically, God's people, the Israelites, are living in the promised land. It's the land God promised to Abraham's family way back in Genesis 12—and some 500 years later, God freed them from slavery (Exodus) so that they could go and settle there (Joshua).

But after finally reaching the land, the Israelites kept worshipping foreign gods, and as a result, God kept letting them be oppressed by foreign powers (the book of Judges). Over time, everything spiralled into more and more violence.

So how are things going for Israel at this point? Not good. And how are things going for Elimelek's family? Not good either.

It's easy to find contextual information if you know where to look. Try:

The Gospel Coalition Bible Commentary — www.thegospelcoalition.org/commentary/
Select the book you're looking for and read the "Invitation" section.

The Bible Project's Book Overview videos — https://bibleproject.com/explore/book-overviews/
Most are only around 10 minutes long.

A decent Study Bible will contain a short introduction for every Bible book too. I use mine regularly!

What's more, the narrator hints that, just like the nation as a whole, Elimelek and Naomi aren't making good choices. In response to the food shortage, they move away from the promised land to live in Moab—an enemy territory where everyone worships false gods. And then their sons marry Moabite women. It's when we're in a tight corner that it's hardest to make the right choice.

When have you found that to be true?

It's a bleak introduction to the story. But this tale of woe is setting the stage for God to come through for Naomi—because God always comes through.

How have you seen God be gracious to you, even when you've made bad choices?

Pray: *Praise God that, despite our mess and our sin, he came through for us in the person of Jesus, to turn our stories around.*

Day 2

Pray: *Ask for God's help to hear and respond to his word.*

As chapter 1 continues, we discover more about two of the book's main characters: Naomi and Ruth.

READ RUTH 1:6-22

How would you describe Naomi? What does she believe about the LORD (v 8-9, 13, 20-21)?

When you see "the LORD" printed in small capitals, as in verse 8, it's not a title; it's standing in for God's personal name, Yahweh. (The Israelites regarded this as too holy even to say out loud—so they would read "the LORD" instead.) The use of God's personal name is usually significant and therefore worth taking notice of!

Naomi knows that God can be kind to people—but she feels that he's not been kind to her. Naomi utters strong words. Her life has hit rock bottom, and she knows where to point the finger: at God himself.

How would you describe Ruth? What might she believe about the LORD (v 16-17)?

How do you think she'd be feeling as she arrives in Bethlehem with Naomi, having left her home behind?

So we've got our two characters. There's Naomi: bitter and empty. And Ruth: a foreign widow without a home (v 9).

We're still only at the beginning of the story. But as the plot develops, God is going to provide a welcome and a home for Ruth and turn Naomi's bitterness into joy. And there are glimmers of God at work even at this stage, even if the characters don't see them. Naomi isn't totally alone—she's got her fiercely loyal daughter-in-law with her. And the barley harvest is just about to begin (v 22)… It's as though the writer is drawing us along, so that we want to find out what happens next.

Have you ever felt like Naomi or Ruth—either now or in the past? Do you know someone who would speak as Naomi does?

What glimmers of God's kindness do you see around you today?

Pray: *Ask for God's help to see and appreciate more of his kindness to you through Jesus. Pray for someone you know who is bitter, empty or afflicted like Naomi; ask God to use you to show his kindness to them.*

Day 3

Pray: *Praise God that he sees you, just as he saw Naomi and Ruth. Ask him to speak into your life today.*

Next, the narrator introduces a third key character in the book. Enter Boaz...

READ RUTH 2:1-23

How would you describe Boaz, based on this chapter?

What does Boaz say about the Lord (v 12)?

Why does Naomi seem excited when Ruth returns (v 20)?

Once again, having a sense of where this book sits in Old Testament history helps us to understand what's going on and what it means. A "guardian-redeemer" isn't a thing in our society (v 20). But for Naomi, and for the first readers of this book in Old Testament Israel, it was a familiar and significant concept. Essentially, if someone found themselves in particular situations of great difficulty, the closest male relative in their family was obliged to look after them.

And here again the story is pointing us forwards. What God did for Ruth and Naomi he does for all his people through his Son. Jesus became part of our human family to redeem us from our great problem: sin. And now everyone—Israelite or foreigner, rich or poor—is invited to come and take refuge under his wings. It's there that we'll find security from danger, provision for our needs and a home in which to rest.

Reread the last part of verse 12 with Jesus in mind. *What do you find comforting about that image?*

What would it look like for you to go all in under God's wings? How might that be costly, as it was for Ruth (v 11)?

Pray: *What sin continues to plague you? Imagine yourself coming under Jesus' wings as you confess them to God. What difficult situations do you find yourself in? Imagine yourself coming under God's wings as you ask for his help.*

Day 4

Pray: *Ask God to thrill your heart with his love for you as you read today.*

Ruth has been gleaning in Boaz's fields for about three months (2:23). But it's temporary work, and the harvest season is almost over. So Naomi is planning to secure Ruth a husband who can provide for her permanently...

That hinges on a law that said that if a man died without children, one of his male relatives should marry his widow in order to carry on the family line (Deuteronomy 25:5-6).

READ RUTH 3:1-18

What is the plan (v 1-4)?

Do things go according to plan (v 5-11)? What's the plot twist in verses 12-13?

It's not entirely clear whether Naomi's intentions are all above board. Even if they are, Ruth is putting herself in a vulnerable position—there's a risk to her person and to her reputation. Then again, this isn't the first time Ruth has done something costly out of love for Naomi.

But Boaz is true to his character. When Ruth asks Boaz to spread the "wings" of his garment over her in verse 9, she uses the same word that he did back in 2:12 to describe God's protection. It's a request to take her into his home as his wife—to be the human means that God will use to take care of her and Naomi.

And wonderfully, Boaz is willing... but only if another, closer relative doesn't want to redeem her himself. Boaz cares deeply about God's law.

Where do we see a glimpse of Jesus in these two characters? Think about...

  • *Ruth's treatment of Naomi.*

  • *Boaz's treatment of Ruth.*

Through Jesus, God has provided you—an outsider— with a home with him. That is thrilling!

How might God be calling you to show these Jesus-like qualities today to the people he's put in your life?

Pray: *Talk to God about all that, and more...*

Day 5

Pray: *You know what to do…*

We're rooting for Ruth and Boaz to get married. But will the other guardian-redeemer get in the way?

READ RUTH 4:1-22

It's a happy ending! And now we've reached the end of the book, we can look back and admire the whole journey.

When we met Naomi in chapter 1, she was bitter, empty and afflicted. *How do we see that reversed?*

When we met Ruth in chapter 1, she was a foreign widow without a home. *How do we see that transformed?*

How does the writer point forward to the rest of the Bible story (v 18-22)? Where is the route to Jesus, do you think?

The book of Ruth is the story of one family—but it's also part of the big story of the people of God. God's desire is to call a people who belong to him—a people who live under his rule, enjoying his blessing, living the good life. In many ways, the reign of King David (v 17, 22) was the closest that Israel got to that vision. But that was just a shadow of what was to come…

At the start of the New Testament, we discover another family tree, or genealogy, that also features Ruth, Boaz, Obed and David (Matthew 1:5-6). It turns out that these characters are links in a chain that leads all the way to King Jesus (v 16). And now, because of him, we too can be part of God's people—a people who find a home under his rule, enjoying his blessing, living the good life.

But in enjoying this big picture, don't miss that the book of Ruth remains a story of one family. That tells you that God cares about you as an individual. He's involved in the details of your life. And because of his lovingkindness, he's weaving the ups and downs together to work all things for your good (Romans 8:28). Your story's not over. But it will end happily: at home with Jesus, all bitterness turned to joy.

Pray: *Thank God for everything you've enjoyed from the book of Ruth.*

The Weekend Page

Once more, either take the weekend to catch up or...

- read Ruth all the way through. What strikes you? Journal your thoughts, write out a prayer in response, or memorise one particular verse.

- read the passage that's going to be preached in your church this Sunday. What did you find interesting? Exciting? Surprising? Confusing?

WEEK 6

Putting It All Together

Introduction

You've been reading the Bible for five whole weeks and have made your way through three complete books. That's excellent progress! This week, we're going to launch into a fourth: the Gospel of Mark.

Mark's Gospel is thought to be the first of the four Gospels in the Bible to be written. It's also the shortest. Mark jumps right into Jesus' arrival on the scene as an adult, and the action flows thick and fast from there.

This is the last week in our quiet time kickstart, so it's time for me to take more of a backseat. This week, we're going to put together everything we've seen so far. We'll ask a variation on the same three basic questions of every passage.

- What: What happens? What's the headline? Are there any surprises? What's the mood or tone of the passage—how does it feel?

- Where: Where does this fit? How does this connect with where we've already been? How does it connect with where things are heading? (Remember, you can answer these questions on two levels: 1) the storyline of the individual book and 2) the storyline of the whole Bible.)

- Why: Why does God want me to hear this? Why is this in the Bible? What did the author want their first readers to do with this? And, downstream of that, what does God want you to do with this?

These three questions should give you a solid start in getting the gold out of any Bible passage, whatever book it's in. That said, not every question will be equally useful for every passage—so if you're not sure what the answer is, don't worry. Remember, the aim isn't to get all the answers right. The aim—as it has been all along—is simply to hear our good God speak as we read his word.

Day 1

Pray: *Thank God that Jesus came into the world to show you who God is. Pray that as you read, you would meet Jesus today.*

The introduction to a book sets the agenda and the tone for everything that follows.

READ MARK 1:1-8

What: What happens? What's the headline? How would you describe the tone or mood of what's happening?

Where: Where is Mark heading with his book (v 1)?

Verse 1 sets our expectations: this book is going to be about Jesus, showing us that he is the Son of God, set apart for a special role. (He's the Messiah, which means "anointed one".) These are big claims! But they're also "good news". We get glimpses of what's good about it in verses 4 and 8—but we'll have to keep reading for the whole picture to unfold.

So that's the direction of travel. But Mark also points back to Israel's past. The Old Testament prophets said that a "voice" would announce the arrival of God's coming (v 3). John the Baptist is that voice. John's unusual dress and diet (v 6) would remind his Jewish hearers of Elijah (2 Kings 1:8), a spiritual giant from

For years I wondered what the footnotes mean when they talk about "manuscripts" (like in v 1). Turns out, we no longer have the original scroll that Mark (or any other ancient author) wrote on. What we do have are copies of copies of copies (and so on) of that scroll. Scholars compare these "manuscripts", and any significant differences between them are flagged in the footnotes. The reassuring thing is that, even with so many to compare, overall the copies are remarkably similar!

their history. But even John is only the warm-up act. He's about to pass the mic to someone so great that John's not even worthy of untying his sandals: someone who can not only forgive us but give us his Holy Spirit.

Why: Why does God want you to hear this?

God has come. Your sins are forgiven. The Spirit is yours.

How does that change your outlook on your day?

Pray: *Spend time marvelling at Jesus' power and worthiness. Repent of your sin. Enjoy his forgiveness.*

Day 2

Pray: *Father God, thank you that your Holy Spirit is with me, ready to show me Jesus in your word. Please help me to hear and respond. Amen.*

In verses 1-8, Mark was building the hype for the character who's about to walk on stage. Here he comes...

READ MARK 1:9-15

What: What happens? What are the headlines? Any surprises?

Where: What connections can you see with where we've been already (v 1 especially)?

Once again, Mark draws some Old Testament comparisons that would have been more obvious to readers back then than they might be to us. After the Israelites left slavery in Egypt, they spent 40 years in the wilderness. When tested there, they disobeyed. They needed someone who could pass the test.

Enter Jesus, who spends 40 days in the wilderness (v 12-13). And when tested, he obeys his Father. He succeeds where Israel failed. He's the King of God's kingdom—the spiritual realm of God's good and just and glorious rule—and he's in the business of admitting new citizens. The wait is over (v 15). We can be part of it now. That is good news!

Why: Why does God want you to hear this? What response does he call for (v 15)?

Pray: *Praise Jesus for who he is. Talk to him about ways in which you want to bring your life increasingly under his rule. And believe afresh the good news: through faith in Jesus, your sins are forgiven, and you too are a child of God, whom he loves.*

Day 3

Pray: *Lord Jesus, thank you that you have good news to proclaim to me today. Help me to hear and respond. Amen.*

Jesus has gone into Galilee (v 14), a region in the north of Israel, "proclaiming the good news". Next we get two snapshots of what that roving ministry looked like.

READ MARK 1:16-28

What: What happens? What are the headlines? Any surprises? What's the response of the people/creatures Jesus meets?

Where: What connections can you see with where we've been already?

Authoritative. That's what describes Jesus here. He calls—fishermen follow. He gives an order—evil spirits depart. He teaches—people sit up and listen. Because Jesus has come with a message from God himself (v 15).

Why: Why does God want me to hear this?

Verse 17 is an invitation to Simon and Andrew to be part of Jesus' new mission in the world. It's not easy, but it's exciting! And today, Jesus continues to invite ordinary people like you and me to join him in his kingdom work.

Pray: *How are you going to respond to Jesus today? Talk to him about your answer.*

Day 4

Pray: *Praise God for who he is and ask him to help you to hear and respond.*

READ MARK 1:29-39

What: What happened? What are the headlines? Any surprises?

Where: What connections can you see with where we've already been? (E.g. how do v 38-39 link back to v 14-15?) What connections can you see with where Mark's Gospel is going? (Spoiler: It ends with Jesus' death and resurrection!)

The theme of Jesus' authority continues (v 31, 34). But Jesus doesn't seem interested in fame and fortune. He's focused on another agenda (v 35-38). He's come to proclaim a message that can heal us of a different, much deeper disease.

Another theme to look out for in Mark is Jesus' identity. Who is Jesus? Mark gave us the short answer in verse 1, but through these stories he's building up a fuller picture. The demons recognise who Jesus is. Mark's unspoken question to the reader is: do you?

Why: Why does God want me to hear this?

Pray: *Talk to God about your answer. Praise Jesus for who he is. Repent and return to his rule. Ask your King for what you need.*

Day 5

Pray: *Praise God for who he is and ask him to help you to hear and respond.*

READ MARK 1:40-45

What: What happens? What's the headline? Any surprises? What's the tone of Jesus' words, do you think?

Where: What connections can you see with where we've been already? What connections can you see with where Mark's Gospel is heading?

Why is Jesus indignant at the man's request? Is he angry to have been asked for help? No: his very next action and words show us that this can't be so. Perhaps instead he's indignant at the effect of sin on a broken world. Or it may be that Jesus was "filled with compassion" (see the NIV footnote).

Either way, Jesus is willing. And he can make us clean. All we have to do is come and ask.

Why: Why does God want me to hear this?

Pray: *Talk to God about your response. Praise. Repent. Ask for what you need.*

You've completed The Quiet Time Kickstart! But your journey through Mark is only beginning... You can keep reading using the plan on page 92.

The Weekend Page

Once more, either take the weekend to catch up or...

- read Mark 1 all the way through. What strikes you? Journal your thoughts, write out a prayer in response, or memorise one particular verse.

- read the passage that's going to be preached in your church this Sunday. What did you find interesting? Exciting? Surprising? Confusing?

8-week Reading Plan:

Mark's Gospel

☐ Mark 2:1-12   ☐ Mark 6:14-29

☐ Mark 2:13-22   ☐ Mark 6:30-44

☐ Mark 2:23 – 3:6   ☐ Mark 6:45-56

☐ Mark 3:7-19   ☐ Mark 7:1-23

☐ Mark 3:20-35   ☐ Mark 7:24-37

☐ Mark 4:1-20   ☐ Mark 8:1-13

☐ Mark 4:21-34   ☐ Mark 8:14-26

☐ Mark 4:35 – 5:20   ☐ Mark 8:27-38

☐ Mark 5:21-43   ☐ Mark 9:1-13

☐ Mark 6:1-13   ☐ Mark 9:14-29

- [ ] Mark 9:30-41
- [ ] Mark 9:42-50
- [ ] Mark 10:1-16
- [ ] Mark 10:17-31
- [ ] Mark 10:32-45

- [ ] Mark 10:46-52
- [ ] Mark 11:1-11
- [ ] Mark 11:12-25
- [ ] Mark 11:27 – 12:12
- [ ] Mark 12:13-27

- [ ] Mark 12:28-37
- [ ] Mark 12:38-44
- [ ] Mark 13:1-37
- [ ] Mark 14:1-11
- [ ] Mark 14:12-26

- [ ] Mark 14:27-42
- [ ] Mark 14:43-65
- [ ] Mark 14:66 – 15:15
- [ ] Mark 15:16-41
- [ ] Mark 15:42 – 16:8

Read This First

Well, read this next! If you want to keep being equipped to read God's word with confidence, then, along with just keeping going with reading God's word, this short book is really helpful. It would make a great follow-up now that you've finished your quiet time kickstart.

thegoodbook.com/read-this-first
thegoodbook.co.uk/read-this-first
thegoodbook.com.au/read-this-first

the good book
COMPANY

At The Good Book Company we are dedicated to helping Christians and local churches grow. We believe that God's growth process always starts with hearing clearly what he has said to us through his timeless and flawless word—the Bible.

Ever since we opened our doors in 1991, we have been striving to produce resources that are biblical, relevant, and accessible. By God's grace, we have grown to become an international publisher, encouraging ordinary Christians of every age and stage and every background and denomination to live for Christ day by day and equipping churches to grow in their knowledge of God, their love for one another, and the effectiveness of their outreach.

Call one of our friendly team for a discussion of your needs or visit one of our local websites for more information on the resources and services we provide.

Your friends at The Good Book Company